Six Ways To Strategic Co

Six Ways To Enjoy This Strategic Coach Book

Text **60 Minutes**	The length of our small books is based on the time in the air of a flight between Toronto and Chicago. Start reading as you take off and finish the book by the time you land. Just the right length for the 21st-century reader.
Cartoons **30 Minutes**	You can also gain a complete overview of the ideas in this book by looking at the cartoons and reading the captions. We find the cartoons have made our Strategic Coach concepts accessible to readers as young as eight years old.
Audio **120 Minutes**	The audio recording that accompanies this book is not just a recitation of the printed words but an in-depth commentary that expands each chapter's mindset into new dimensions. Download the audio at **strategiccoach.com/go/abcmodel**
Video **30 Minutes**	Our video interviews about the concepts in the book deepen your understanding of the mindsets. If you combine text, cartoons, audio, and video, your understanding of the ideas will be 10x greater than you would gain from reading only. Watch the videos at **strategiccoach.com/go/abcmodel**
Scorecard **10 Minutes**	Score your ABC Model Breakthrough mindset at **strategiccoach.com/go/abcmodel**. First, score yourself on where you are now, and then fill in where you want to be a year from now.
ebook **1 Minute**	After absorbing the fundamental ideas of the ABC Model Breakthrough concept, you can quickly and easily share them by sending the ebook version to as many other individuals as you desire. Direct them to **strategiccoach.com/go/abcmodel**

Creative Team:

Adam Morrison

Kerri Morrison

Hamish MacDonald

Shannon Waller

Jennifer Bhatthal

Victor Lam

Margaux Yiu

Christine Nishino

Willard Bond

Peggy Lam

The ABC Model Breakthrough

We all have activities that irritate us, bore us, and drain our energy. The problem is thinking that this is just a necessary part of life and business. In this book, I show you a simple process to shed those unwanted activities to not only free yourself up to concentrate on what fascinates and motivates you but to strengthen your team as well.

Imagine spending your workdays doing only what you find endlessly fascinating. This is a reality for entrepreneurs who adopt The ABC Model.

Printed in Toronto, Canada. The Strategic Coach Inc., 33 Fraser Avenue, Suite 201, Toronto, Ontario, M6K 3J9.

If you would like further information about The Strategic Coach® Program or other Strategic Coach® services and products, please telephone 416.531.7399 or 1.800.387.3206.

ISBN Paperback: 978-1-64085-860-2
ISBN eBook: 978-1-64085-861-9
Library of Congress Control Number: 2019912500

Contents

Introduction
Simplifying Is The Only Solution
You leave behind all complicated time management systems that undermine your confidence and waste your energy.

Over the 43 years that I've been coaching entrepreneurs, every year or so a new time management system is introduced into the market, each one being hailed as "the definitive time management system."

These new systems are generally directed to corporate executives, corporate managers, and corporate workers. They're geared to people who don't have much choice about what they're going to work on, who they're going to work with, or what kind of situations they're going to be in.

In other words, these books aren't geared toward entrepreneurs — individuals who start their own businesses and go out and create their own opportunities.

Instead, they normalize a lack of choice in people's lives and in what they do. They replace the feeling you'd get from making really great choices with a sense of great busyness. They try to make you proud of how busy you are, but the truth is that busyness actually tends to undermine people's confidence and waste their energy.

Stop treating yourself like a machine.
These time management systems let individuals believe they should perform like machines do, with consistent action all day long.

Something I've noticed about busy work is that it doesn't make people more creative or more productive, and it certainly doesn't make them more satisfied.

Entrepreneurs choose to be entrepreneurs with all the risks and uncertainties that go along with this path precisely because they want to live a work life that is creative, productive, and satisfying.

There are many entrepreneurs who think, "I'm going to use this new time system because if any of the large corporations use it, then it must be really good." But it's not geared whatsoever to their choice of lifestyle. It's not geared to the kind of working environment that entrepreneurs set up, that they and the people who work for them enjoy, and within which they expand their creativity, achievement, and sense of satisfaction.

Complexity is just a way of thinking.

If you master the busyness with these time management systems, and just pack your schedule with activities, your life is going to become incredibly more complex. These advertised solutions claim that this is just the way the world works, that things are complex and complicated, and that you should just figure out how to best perform within this complexity. But this is not the way it has to be.

The first thing you have to do to get a handle on time is to stop treating yourself like a machine. Realize that all the complexity that makes up modern work life—dealing with hundreds of emails, being forced into multitasking, and having your life filled up with meetings—is just a way of thinking about things.

You don't have to think about work in this way at all.

Simplifying your life in a single hour.

There's an entirely different way of thinking about your time and activity. It's called The ABC Model, and I've been developing it over my more than 40 years of working with people who aren't trained to be busy in the normal organizational sense, but rather are trying to be extremely effective and to have a sense of expansion and growth.

Your shift to this new way of thinking about time will suddenly and permanently simplify things for you, and it will happen in the time it takes to read this book.

This new way of looking at how you spend your time can replace virtually the entire literature of time management, and it's just one idea and one diagram. Once you grasp it, your view of the life you've led, the life you're living now, and the life you're looking forward to leading is going to shift tremendously.

A multiplier power you've always had.

By their nature, entrepreneurs want a life based not on the general narrative that applies to the majority, but on a specific narrative that has to do with their unique capabilities and opportunities, and an entirely different way of approaching the marketplace.

We can look at time from a completely different viewpoint. Once you understand The ABC Model, you'll realize that you already have everything inside you that's necessary to instantly master this. There's a power you've always had but has never been identified as being important. In fact, it's usually seen as being a hindrance to fitting in with the general time system. As you'll see, it's based on a way of responding to things that's largely discouraged in big systems.

The only thing that's been lacking is that you haven't noticed you have this power. I'm not asking you to learn something entirely new. I'm simply asking you to take seriously something you already have.

Remarkable progress 90 days from now.

From the time we're children, we're given the message that we just have to do some things we hate, and that if we get good enough at them, eventually we'll like doing them.

This almost never happens. What happens is that you go from hating the activity to hating yourself, since you can't change the activity. You deaden yourself so that you stop feeling those negative emotions about the work you're doing.

Once you read this short book, you can start experiencing the most energizing progress of your life in just three months.

I've seen entrepreneurs grasp The ABC Model concept and realize they can start doing things this way immediately. One entrepreneur was spending 25 hours a week doing bidding proposals. He hated doing them, and they were negatively affecting his weekends and his home life, but he felt he was the only one who could do them.

Following our model, that entrepreneur has now gotten back about 1,000 work hours a year, is doing better work, and is loving the work he's doing. It all came from one decision, one communication, and one action.

Chapter 1
Three Circle Breakthrough
You continually organize your past, present, and future by transforming all of your activity according to three kinds of emotional responses.

In the typical time management book, tasks and activities are treated like products on an assembly line to be dealt with. How you feel about the activities isn't considered because the vast majority of people have no choice about the activities they're doing. If anything, these systems just try to make long suffering into short suffering by showing you how to do the things you dislike more quickly and efficiently.

But if something isn't appropriate for you—and this includes people and certain types of situations, in addition to activities—more and more, nothing about it will be appropriate for you. When you look back at previous negative work experiences, chances are you were simply doing the wrong activity.

I want you to become very alert and responsive to how you feel about activities that you've done, that you're doing, and that you will do, and start to sort your activities according to three kinds of emotional responses.

Everything you do in one diagram.
The first thing to understand is that there can only be one solution in dealing with complexity, and that's simplicity. What usually takes up pages and pages of description

about how a time system works has to be brought down to the simplest possible thing, which I communicate in one diagram. A single diagram can be worth a thousand pages, and a single diagram properly understood can be worth more than 50 strategies or 50 procedures.

The entire time system and activity system we're introducing here consists of one diagram, which consists of three circles: a big circle labeled A, a medium-sized circle labeled B, and a small circle labeled C. The small circle is inside of the medium circle, which is inside of the big circle.

We're giving you a growth plan for the rest of your life in this single diagram.

Each circle is a familiar experience.

There are a lot of people who make their living off of complexity because they want their clients to need their help over long periods of time. But I've based my career on allowing entrepreneurs to expand their entrepreneurial freedom, and I'm happy to get something across in a short time if it can be done. I don't believe that modern life has to be complex.

Each of the three circles in our simple diagram represents an experience that's very familiar to you, that you've almost certainly been having for as long as you can remember.

Here are the three words to describe the three types of experiences: Irritating, Okay, and Fascinating.

Irritating, Okay, and Fascinating.

Can you think of things you've done that you found irritating, things you've done that were just okay, and things you've done that you were fascinated by? Every entrepreneur I've asked these questions to has been able to relate each of those feelings to an endless amount of experiences they've had in their lives.

On almost any day, you can experience all three of these: irritating, which is very negative, okay, which is neutral, and fascinating, which is positive.

There are, of course, other kinds of emotional responses you can have, but if you understand and get a handle on these three as an anchor, you'll be able to sort out all the others.

Motivating yourself in three permanent ways.

There have always been things you've found irritating, that currently irritate you, and that, if you continue doing them, will continue to irritate you.

Activities that are merely okay are what you might also think of as treadmill activities. They don't really irritate you, but you don't get an energy jump as a result of doing them. When it comes to these types of activities, people might normalize them by thinking, "These are just things we have to do when we go to work."

Then there's fascinating. These are the activities you love and never get tired of doing.

If you think about it, each of these experiences acts as a motivator in a different way. Once you tell the truth that you find something irritating, you're motivated to stop the irritation. Once you realize that some things you do are just okay and don't have much value to you, you think of them as kind of a dead spot in your life and are motivated to move on from them.

When you recognize something you do as being fascinating, you're motivated to continually enlarge it and expand it and take the fascination to a higher level.

You've already done this many times.
I have a hypothesis that you've already been using The ABC Model throughout your life without knowing it.

At the times in your life when you've grown as an individual, especially if you're an entrepreneur who's become more successful in the marketplace, I'm willing to bet that you've been eliminating irritating tasks and activities, delegating the ones that are just okay, and expanding the time you're spending doing things you find fascinating.

You've always had these emotions, so if you're doing much better and producing bigger results today, it's because you've already made a lot of shifts based on them.

You just didn't realize you were doing it.

So, what we're doing now is putting a name to each time you've made a significant shift and moved closer to a life where you love everything you're doing. I want to show you how you did that and the power of paying attention to your emotional responses. I want to give you the framework of the three circles to organize your thinking so that it can become a planning tool that helps you make more significant shifts every 90 days.

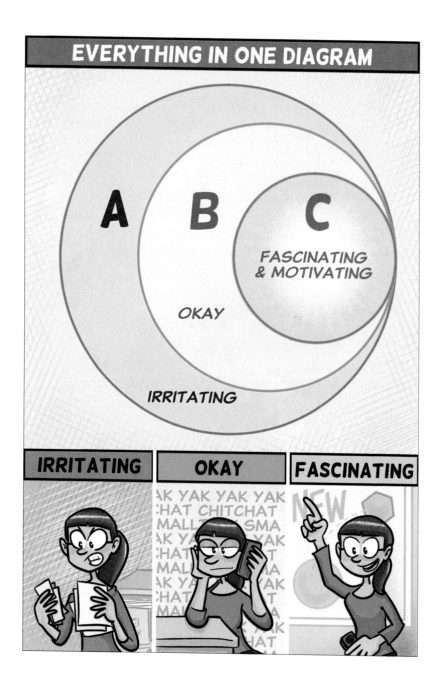

Chapter 2
Emotionally Alert And Decisive

You're increasingly alert to what your emotions are telling you about the best improvements you can make right now.

Unlike some people I've met, the question of life after death doesn't interest me. What I focus on is life *before* death.

If you deaden your emotions in order to, say, just accept your situation without feeling the need to make any changes, then you don't have life before death.

I want you to expand your entrepreneurial freedom, and one of the big freedoms is being alert to your emotions, using them as a guide to what you *will* do and what you *won't* do.

My goal is for you to be constantly expanding the things you love doing, which will totally transform your time management and results.

Let your emotions be your guide.

We all have emotions, and experiencing some of these emotions drains our energy, and experiencing other emotions increases our energy.

Your effectiveness, creativity, productivity, and satisfaction with what you're doing are a function of your energy level. The energy levels of those around you are also a factor, but to start with, let's focus on yours.

Consider an activity you're doing. Do you love it, hate it, or feel it's just okay? Don't dissect the emotion—just take it at face value. It's important to trust your emotions as you pay more and more attention to them and let them guide you.

All thinking focused on improvement.
Use your best decision-making, communication, and action to shift all of your time from negative and neutral activities to increasingly positive ones.

At the end of each quarter, your ABC Model approach to your work will be better than it was 90 days before, and over the following 90 days, it's going to continue improving.

The amount of your time that you spend on fascinating activities is going to keep growing, and this is because the more you use the system, the more your intelligence about it increases. Your sensitivity to your emotions is going to become more and more finely tuned as time goes on. You'll notice when certain fascinating activities become just okay for you, and when certain neutral activities slip down into the category of irritating.

This system is never static. You'll always be improving, checking in at regular intervals to evaluate how things have changed, and that in itself will lead you to think of new improvements you can make. You'll be constantly shifting.

Eliminate everything that irritates.
We want to completely eliminate the "irritating" category in our lives. There are no acceptable irritations. No irritation can ever justify itself.

A lot of people put up with irritating activities by telling themselves that no job can be enjoyable all of the time.

But you need to shift away from that mindset. The goal is to move all of your time out of the A and B categories (Irritating and Okay) and into C (Fascinating).

Start by identifying and listing every activity you currently do that frustrates, annoys, confuses, and demoralizes you. These are the activities you'll focus on eliminating. Every one of them.

There's a truth telling that has to enter here. Don't suffer in silence when it comes to irritating. It doesn't do you any good, and you're not doing anyone else any good either. There's no value in putting up with irritating activities. There may be periods where for a day or two you have to do things that are irritating, but you should have a deadline for when that's no longer going to be necessary because then you get the benefit of having a future without it on your schedule.

Delegate everything that's just okay.

Okay activities can usually be described as having some valuable result but are predictable and repetitive for you. In spending time on these activities, you won't have any new thoughts or go through any new experiences. They are what they are, and there's no reason to think they're ever going to get any better.

You don't want these activities to disappear—they're necessary to your business—but you don't want to keep doing them yourself. The best thing to do is to delegate them or automate them.

With any okay activity, you can find someone who's better at it than you are and who finds doing the activity fascinating. Everyone on the planet has a range from irritating to fascinating that's different from everyone else's. An activity that's predictable and repetitive for you will be new and fascinating for someone else. Anybody who's energetically engaged with their work is going to be innovative, so there are very few areas where someone who's fascinated by an area of activity won't be able to constantly make improvements that keep them endlessly engaged.

Another option is automation. This starts with delegation and then goes further. Once the best way of doing something is determined, and it's not going to change, it's ripe for automating.

Continually expand fascinating time.

A activities are for eliminating, B are for delegating and automating, and C are for expanding. You can make a commitment right now to fill your time only with activities that are increasingly fascinating and motivating to you by freeing yourself up from everything else.

You can do this with regular check-ups and by making new plans. It's a complete time system that goes on forever, and it's guided by your emotions toward activities.

Every 90 days is a good time to make shifts and tell the truth about how you feel about all your activities. With the new truths you'll have at the end of every 90-day period, you'll do some new planning and new shifting.

Take a moment now to just imagine being fascinated and motivated most of the time. That's what you're going to be constantly moving toward if you make the commitment to getting that result for yourself. It's going to be a lot of work in using this system, and nobody else can do that work for you, but the results are worth it.

Chapter 3
Eliminate Everything Irritating

You accept that anything that irritates you will always be a waste of your energy — and you immediately work to eliminate it.

Your time and energy are precious, and irritating activities are never going to become fascinating to you. Once you accept this, you can get out of the habit of thinking that you'll just get used to things that irritate you. It won't happen.

As soon as you tell the truth to yourself that an activity is irritating, the only thing you can do to improve things is to eliminate it.

Don't get used to it. Get rid of it.

I always have a list of things that irritate me, but I know there's a time limit on everything on that list. If it's on the list, it has a death sentence. It's going to be altered.

My destination is all Cs (Fascinating), and every A (Irritating) is a temporary obstacle to getting to a C. My focus is on constantly expanding, deepening, and improving my area of fascinating activities. An A is the raw material for a C. Irritating activities are things to be transformed.

Things that always drain you.
You have to give up all wishes, hopes, and fantasies that things that irritated you in the past, that irritate you even more right now, will become enjoyable in the future.

Sticking with something that irritates you is denying the basis of your uniqueness. You won't be able to get a grasp on what makes you unique without telling the truth about what gives you energy and what drains you of energy. How could you get a handle on it if you don't have any emotional basis for clearly identifying what your uniqueness actually is? Specific irritations are incredibly valuable information. They tell you, "Over there, not here. Stay away from here."

Things that irritate you are good for teaching, but they're not good for experiencing. If you know something is irritating, don't go there.

Don't expect that there's going to be some kind of magical transformation without your coming to grips with something, making a decision, and taking an action. This is for your growth. If you don't have any plans to grow, then by all means, put up with everything you're putting up with, but if you have plans to grow, this is the road by which you grow as an individual.

Freeing yourself forever.

The goal here is to free yourself forever from every irritating kind of action for the rest of your life. Just visualizing having that kind of freedom in your life will immediately generate energy.

As soon as you tell the truth about an irritation, you'll get a huge amount of energy back because you can then give the activity an expiration date. You may have to stay with it for a few more months as you make the necessary changes in your life and business to get rid of it, but you know that the irritating activity won't be in your life forever.

It's also important to communicate with others about your feelings. This is a very social model—if you're isolated, you can't do anything with it. You have to see the possibility that there might be somebody who would find fascinating this activity that's irritating to you. You have to believe that there's someone who would love the opportunity to take this activity off your hands.

The big breakthrough here is that it's okay to tell the truth about being irritated by things and to eliminate them. A lot of people deaden themselves because they feel that the irritating situation is going to be perpetual and there's no way out of it. Telling the truth brings you back to life. Instead of just being annoyed at life or circumstances, you use irritation as part of a transformational process for your growth. You'll recognize when you're irritated, and you'll do something about it.

Start by telling the truth.

Every time you tell the truth that something's irritating, you're halfway to a solution.

But there's work. A shift like this requires a shift of under-standing, a shift of activity, and a shift of agreement. There's teamwork involved. But you'll never start this process if you don't start by telling the truth.

If you've never done this before, it's extraordinarily hard. You might think that you don't have the right to do this. People get themselves into a box, and if it's your first time attempting to get out of the box, it can be difficult. But starting by telling the truth is the only way out, and it will get easier after that first time, and even easier each time you do it.

Every decision creates new energy.

Even before an irritation is eliminated, your acknowledgment of it pulls energy out of it. Right away, you free up the irritation from permanence and from acceptance. You've said, "This isn't acceptable, and as soon as possible, it will be eliminated." Part of the irritation was that you felt you were stuck with it.

And it's not just for your own benefit; irritated people are hard to be around. Their irritation impacts teamwork, communication, and relationships. Most of us want to stay away from irritated people.

Everything goes to Fascinating.

A fascinated person, on the other hand, is great to be around. They're magnetic, positive, and always innovating because they've freed themselves from everything that had been bogging them down and wasting their time.

By adopting this model, you're permitting yourself to look at everything in your life as being in one of three circles, and you're getting the most out of reducing the number of activities you find irritating and just okay and liberating that time to move increasingly into your ever-expanding zone of fascinating activities.

You're using emotions and energy as the sensor that tells you what's the right direction for you to go in and what's the wrong direction to go in, allowing you to live in a more and more fascinating world.

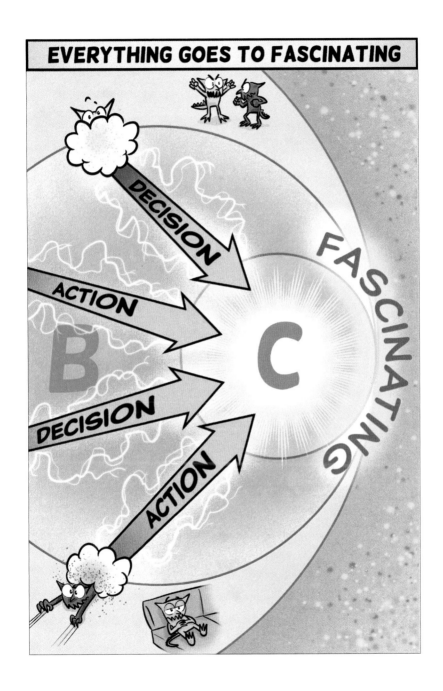

Chapter 4
Delegating "Okay"

You recognize that any situation that merely has "okay" energy is always a great project for permanent delegation and automation.

It's important that you're able to recognize when an activity you do is just an "okay" one.

Okay is neutral. It doesn't irritate you, but it doesn't excite you either.

Even though it might not make you feel a strong negative emotion, it isn't worth your time and energy. Give yourself permission to free up all of your time and energy for activities you find fascinating and motivating.

Things no longer exciting.

There are growth stages in the career of every entrepreneur. Your first growth stage is the most exciting one you've ever had. At this stage, even though the activity may not really click with who you are or where you're going in your career, the first money coming in and the first challenges you face can be extraordinarily fascinating and motivating.

But you're going to grow beyond it, and once you can see the next growth stage, the one you're in no longer seems quite as exciting. You're going to become more and more aware of activities that are time-consuming but no longer stimulate your thinking. The higher stage will offer you more time in the activities you find most fascinating.

Delegate and go higher.

A key reason why people get tired of their occupation or profession is that they haven't really jumped to higher growth stages in many years. They've gotten into a routine where they achieve credibility, respect, and a solid income, but there's nothing new or exciting about it. They're not being tested or challenged to develop new capabilities.

Growing to the next level will mean setting bigger goals and going into new areas of activity where you'll be back to the beginning in terms of a learning curve.

To grow to the next level, two things have to happen:
1. Create higher goals for yourself so that you're back in a place you find fascinating.
2. Delegate the activities you've been doing that no longer fascinate you.

Someone's next big step.

Every okay activity can be handed over to someone who loves doing it and is better skilled at it.

A lot of people hesitate to delegate their okay activities because they think of these jobs as grunt work that no one else would be interested in. But the exact opposite is true.

There aren't any "bad" jobs—there's simply work that's inappropriate for you. Every activity that you find just okay is perfect for somebody, and they'll love doing it.

When you take your next big step and delegate an activity, you're making it possible for the person who takes it over to take their own next big step. It wasn't exciting for you, and that's fine, but it will be for them.

All of us on the planet are at different stages of our growth. Your moving up from something okay to something fascinating allows someone else to move up from something they find okay to something they find fascinating. By making this move and vacating a position you no longer want to be in, it actually helps others too.

Teamwork creates technology.

An aspect of delegation that's often overlooked is automation. Automation is a form of delegation where you have something that's so predictable and repetitive, you can put it into technological form.

It's a seamless progression from teamwork to technology. I think of technology as teamwork that's so guaranteed to get consistent results, it can be automated.

Automating processes is the best thing to do in a lot of cases, because while humans are good for a lot of things, two things we're not good for are predictability and repetition. This is because we have a tendency to wonder and to innovate, but machines aren't built to do those things.

For some activities, it may be that you want to be able to predict repetitive performance. These are best suited to machines, which we can count on to not have minds of their own. We don't want our technological infrastructures to have higher aspirations!

To a certain extent, the challenge of automation is that it requires humans to do only activities that fascinate them. After all, it's not worth paying someone to do work that a machine can do and would be better at doing.

The bar is being raised for the whole human race, which

has been going on for a couple of centuries now, where we're asking for a higher level of engagement, a higher level of participation in our work.

Making sure you're doing something that fascinates you, which is a strictly human thing, might be the only way to protect yourself from automation.

Freed up time and thinking.

Delegation and automation are the surest ways to boost your own creativity and productivity. They not only free up your time, but also free up your thinking.

Tightly scheduled entrepreneurs can't innovate. You need some slack in your system to transform yourself, to be able to step back and actually look at what you're doing. You can't be focused on working non-stop.

You need to look at what you're doing, consider it all, and recognize what fascinates you and what irritates you. Then delegate or automate everything that doesn't fascinate you to free yourself up.

Getting rid of irritating activities isn't enough. For some people, doing an okay activity might seem like a great relief because they've been operating totally in the irritating zone, but don't just go from irritating to okay.

Go from irritating to fascinating, and from okay to fascinating. There's only one destination in the ABC system and that's C.

Chapter 5

Expanding Fascinating (And Motivating)

You identify, integrate, and continually expand every activity in your life that will increasingly fascinate and motivate you in the future.

If you ask someone whom they've found most compelling in their lives, the answer will invariably be people who are fascinated with what they're doing.

It can be hard to compare ourselves to people we find compelling, especially if they're star athletes or entertainers, because we think what we're seeing is something special about the individual.

It isn't, though. It's something about the individual's relationship to their work. They're fully engaged and immersed in the activity, and they only got to where they are by being fascinated by activities they're extraordinarily good at — which they became extraordinarily good at because they followed their fascination.

It's time to examine what's in your life that really fascinates you and where you'd like to spend more and more of your time.

For as long as you can remember.
The things you like doing most right now were likely evident when you were a child.

What fascinates and motivates me now at seventy-three, I was onto when I was seven years old. It was conversation. I loved conversations in which I was essentially igno-rant and was just using questions to pull out other people's experiences so I could learn from them.

I had this nailed down when I was seven, but I got talked out of it, or else didn't see the importance of it. You don't have contextual understanding when you're seven years old. It takes quite a long time. I knew I was fascinated with the activity; I just didn't think one could build a life around having conversations.

After more than 40 years of coaching entrepreneurs, I know I was wrong.

Things you find easiest to do.
I believe that what you find fascinating and motivating is formed at birth. And because you take to this activity nat-urally and because it's so enjoyable for you, it's also the activity you find easiest to do. You don't even think about it.

If an activity becomes too easy, it can become boring and slip down into the okay category. It's important to stay challenged, and you'll do this by continually taking on bigger and bigger projects within your area of fascinating activities.

In the 1950s and 1960s, when I was growing up, I don't remember anyone saying that liking the work you were doing was part of the deal. People used to believe there was a virtue in putting up with something you didn't like doing and that the only important thing was that you had a job. It's only recently in world history that people have the relative abundance and freedom to entertain the thought that it's important to love what you do.

This is what The ABC Model is all about. You're making definite judgments about what's irritating, what's okay, and what's fascinating, and moving the time you're spending in A and B into C, where things are the most fascinating, most enjoyable, and easiest.

All of your happiest achievements.

Even when it comes to your achievements in life, you can probably identify ones that were irritating, ones that were just okay, and ones that were fascinating. If you look back at your lifetime and tell the truth about your experiences, you'll see that there was unhappiness that went along with some of your achievements, and there are some achievements you don't feel much pride or satisfaction in.

The achievements that were hands-down the happiest and most satisfying ones for you were the ones that involved the activities that still fascinate and motivate you now. Don't be fooled by success in your areas of irritating and okay. It's still time to let those activities go.

The more you do, the more you want.

You can't get enough of doing the activities you find the most fascinating. When you start focusing on them, you'll very quickly start to see ways that you can rearrange your time in order to spend even more time focused on them.

Other people also benefit from your doing what's fascinating to you. We love being in the presence of people who find the activity they're doing fascinating because those people are happy. They have great skill and, generally, they're being creative because they're testing out their fascinating activities in entirely new situations. They're curious and always on an exploratory path.

There's a sense of excitement about them, and we're fascinated by excitement. We love to see people engaged in asking questions that haven't been asked before. We're willing to spend large sums of money on what they're offering, partly because they're going into new territory, doing things that haven't been done before in that way.

You can never do too much of this.
When you're working in your area of fascinating activities, it's inherently motivating, and you can never exhaust your growth.

This is certainly the case for me right now. I'm noticing the sharp distinction between the path I'm taking into my future, where I'm thoroughly enjoying my daily activities and can never see a point at which I'll want to stop, and the retirement route that others are taking in order to leave behind activities they don't really like. It's much better to leave behind those activities now without retiring.

There might be a risky period that occurs when you move your time into fascinating and motivating and don't necessarily get an immediate response and reward from doing it. But keep moving forward. Once you're through this period, you'll have crossed the threshold into total belief in your own instinct, where you no longer question your feelings, be they feelings of irritation, neutrality, or fascination.

Also, keep in mind that you can do this by degrees. Just keep moving and shifting your time, eliminating one irritating activity or delegating one okay activity to spend more time in an activity that you recognize as being fascinating. Make shifts every quarter, and in one year, two years, three years, you'll be living a life in which every day is fascinating.

Chapter 6
Tell The Truth Every 90 Days
You use each three-month period of your life to move any time spent in "irritating" and "okay" into the "fascinating" zone.

A lot of business is done in terms of quarters. A period of 90 days gives you a chance to renew your commitment, complete a goal, or learn something new.

In The ABC Model system, we think in terms of 100 quarters. If you move two or three "irritating" things and two or three "okay" things into "fascinating" every quarter for 100 quarters, your life will improve incredibly in those 25 years.

Measure yourself every quarter.
Using The ABC Model is one of the most productive things anyone can do. Every change in this process starts with your saying, "I don't want to do this anymore." A quarter from then, one way or another, you won't be doing that activity any longer. You'll have shifted how you're managing your time, and it will all be done on the basis of emotion.

The power of The ABC Model is that you'll know for sure whether it's working because you'll have either a negative emotion related to your activities or a positive one, and there's no mistaking it.

Nobody can tell you that you shouldn't find something irritating. Someone who isn't too sure of themselves or who can be overwhelmed by someone else's opinion can actually talk themselves out of their own emotional responsiveness. But if you don't tell the truth about how you feel, there's no chance for this process to work. Nobody else's truth can override your own.

Everything is A, B, or C.
Everything you've ever done, are doing now, and will ever do in the future can be understood as irritating, okay, or fascinating. It can be—and is—this simple. Everything's in the confines of A, B, or C. There is no D.

This emotion-based system transcends factors like skill level. If you're really good at something but feel neutral about it, then it's in B. How you feel about it is what's important.

As an entrepreneur, you've chosen to take total control of your time. Most people, for one reason or another, go to work for organizations where their time is controlled by others. But for those who own their own companies, you've put yourself in the position where it's possible to decide for yourself how you'll spend your time, and part of this is making sure you love what you do.

One destination for all your improvement.
There's only one definition for every kind of future improvement: *anything that moves your time and activity from A and B into C.*

This can relate to dozens of different kinds of activities in your life, and in each case, it has everything to do with your emotions. You'll always know for sure if something is fascinating to you. And if something you're doing isn't fascinating, you know where the time you're spending on it needs to move.

The more you reinforce what's fascinating to you, the more motivated you'll be to shift time away from everything that isn't. If you don't reinforce what's fascinating, there's a danger that you'll start to think of okay or even irritating activities as good enough. The more anchored you become in C, the quicker and more practical you'll become about eliminating, delegating, or automating every A and B activity.

Your standards keep going up.
With The ABC Model, you'll never run out of new ways to make quarterly improvements because your standards for what's fascinating will keep increasing. Things you once found fascinating will eventually become just okay for you, and things you felt were just fine will start to feel annoying.

The more you go through this process of shifting your time into fascinating activities, the more you're going to interact with the world in a more interesting way. It isn't just you in a room by yourself. More and more, you'll be doing what fascinates you, and you'll keep testing it out in new situations in the world, with new relationships, with new challenges, and with new activities.

While your standards about what constitutes fascinating keep going up, your standards for what's irritating will become more finely tuned. This expands to activities throughout your life.

For instance, I've found that I stop reading books sometimes after getting just a few pages in, whereas before I might have stuck it out even though I found it irritating. And I've walked out of more movies in recent years than I did before adopting this model. I no longer have patience for things that don't fascinate me. My time is valuable and better spent elsewhere.

Freeing yourself up for more.

In adopting this model, the first thing you have to do is look inward and tell the truth about how you're experiencing life. If you do this and make shifts every 90 days, the people around you will also be greatly rewarded for your transformation. Fascinated people are great to be around.

Much of this process involves freedom. It's *freedom from* things you don't like doing and *freedom to* do the things you love. A lot of people are very clear on what they'd like to be freed up from, but they're not as clear on what they'd like to be freed up to do.

It takes more responsibility to say what it is you want to be freed up to do, because the world is supplying half the stimulus when it's an unpleasant experience and you want to be freed up from it. But *freedom to* is 100 percent your input because the world can't tell you what you want to be freed up to do. It takes a lot more courage, commitment, and growth to say what you want to be spending your time doing than it does to say what you *don't* want to do.

If you don't reinforce what C is and define what it is you want to be spending your time doing, you won't make any movement from A and B. There won't be enough motivation. There won't be enough payoff. You have to keep increasing the payoff for moving from A and B to C because, otherwise, you'll run out of incentive. You'll decide that things are "good enough" despite irritations and boredom.

In order to be motivated to free yourself up from where you are, you have to know where you're going.

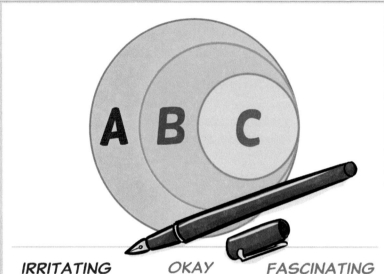

IRRITATING	OKAY	FASCINATING
- ENERGY-DRAINING	- REPETITIVE	- EXCITING
- ISOLATING	- COMPETENT	- CHALLENGING
- OVERWHELMING	- STANDARDIZED	- SURPASSING
- FAILING	- REQUIRED	- ACCELERATING
- DEMORALIZING	- HABITUAL	- INNOVATING

BREAK-THROUGH

- VISION
- COMMITMENT
- FOCUS
- ALIGNMENT
- TEAMWORK
- ACHIEVEMENT
- TRANSFORMATION

Chapter 7
Growth Formula For Everyone

You continually master The ABC Model for yourself while also teaching an increasing number of others how to do it.

Pursuing what's unique about ourselves is actually what creates enormous value out in the world. By focusing only on what you love and find fascinating, you'll do all sorts of things that are of great benefit to other people. And the more you pay attention to what's going on with yourself, the keener your ability becomes to pick up on what's going on with others.

You're transforming your thinking in adopting The ABC Model for yourself as an entrepreneur, but for true growth to happen, you'll need to extend the benefits of the system to everyone in your organization.

You'll want this for everybody.

As more and more of your time and activity are spent in your area of fascinating and motivating, it's natural for you to want this for everybody else, and it makes total sense that it should happen.

You'll never run out of opportunities to be fascinated, and neither will anyone else. There is an abundance of opportunities, not a scarcity. By being more fascinated, you're not making someone else more miserable. It's not a zero-sum game. It's a total plus game.

If everyone in a company goes through their own ABC

Model exercise every quarter, all of the team leaders will know what each team member finds irritating and where each team member can make a jump to something fascinating. That's crucial information for a leader in any organization to know. Why wouldn't you want to free people up from irritating activities and let them engage more and more with what fascinates them? They'll produce better work and be passionate about doing it.

Immediate understanding and action.

I was giving a presentation to a group of entrepreneurs, and I took them through The ABC Model. At the end of the presentation, one of the attendees said to me that he had never before taken a look at his activities and articulated which ones he loved and which ones he hated. He owned an ad agency, and for the first time, he admitted to himself that he hated working with the creative people—the writers and artists. He loved interacting with the clients, but wanted nothing to do with the creative people.

He had been talking for years with someone who knew how to run a creative department, and after going through The ABC Model and writing down the activities he hated doing, he called this person up and he agreed to come in and take over the department. For ten years, this entrepreneur had been feeling this irritation but only after telling the truth and writing it down did he decide to finally take action.

The goal of The ABC Model is to free as much of your time as possible from things that make you feel negative or neutral so that you can spend more time doing what you love. The model is so simple that anyone can understand it quickly.

For the people you work with, it can be even easier for them if you've made the transformation first. Your improved motivation and productivity will set an example for them and encourage them to make their own improvements.

Biggest, fastest jump in teamwork.
When your whole team adopts The ABC Model, your teamwork with everyone else gets better in dozens of ways, with each individual taking daily initiative.

But if you don't do it yourself first, your team members won't do it. Once you've done The ABC Model exercise, you can sit down with them and show them what you want to get freed up from and what you want to get freed up to do. You can explain that while you're going to be the first one doing it, you want all of them to go through the same exercise every quarter and tell the truth about what they want to be freed up from and what they want to be freed up to do.

Let them know that as the entrepreneur and owner of the company, you're committed to helping them every quarter to make the shifts they want to make, but first they have to look at your ABCs and help you to get freed up. Explain your problems and ask how they'd solve them.

This is a beautiful kind of teamwork, because you're determining how you can make this positive shift, with the promise that you'll support the same thing happening for them every quarter.

Everybody helps everybody grow.
I'm now very sensitive and responsive to team members in my company saying they don't like doing something. I want everybody in Strategic Coach shifting from A to C and from B to C every quarter. That's how we've grown the company.

It requires that everybody tell the truth about it and be willing to work practically to make it happen. It might not happen exactly the way they want it to this quarter, but it will be taken seriously and there will be commitment to see it happen.

You'll be surprised by how easy it is for each person in your company to contribute to greater cooperation and creativity. Humans, if they're guaranteed the same treatment, are wholeheartedly enthusiastic about helping others experience greater freedom.

We want to move more of our time into our area of fascinating and motivating activities, and we understand that everyone else is of the same mindset.

Trading activities will be a big part of this process, as whenever someone stops doing an activity that falls under A or B for them, that newly vacated position is a potential C activity for someone else. Everyone at the company will become alert to and creative about opportunities for themselves and others to trade up to something they find more fascinating.

Your growing ABC organization.

When you get a whole group taking this on, you see amazing shifts because it becomes a mindset: We're in The ABC Model. We're an ABC organization. This is how we operate.

The organization you've always dreamed about will continually become a growing reality, with progress taking place every quarter.

YOU'LL WANT THIS FOR EVERYBODY

Chapter 8
100 ABC Quarterly Jumps
Your excitement about this quarter's ABC Model Breakthrough increases your commitment to doing this for 25 years.

The ABC Model leads to a transformation every time you go through the exercise. When you sit down and examine how much time and activity you're spending in each of the three emotional zones, you're able to identify specific actions you can take to improve the way you're allocating your time.

Once you see that there's no reason why you should continue to do a particular A or B activity when your time and energy could be moved to C, you'll be immediately motivated to make decisions and take actions that shift your time.

I've found that a quarter is a good time period to get through five significant changes that will have you spending more time in your area of "fascinating," and a 25-year framework gives you enough space and time to achieve your biggest goals. Looking at your quarterly activity in the framework of 25 years, it's 100 sets of jumps in your ability to operate within the fascinating zone.

Things just keep getting better.
With The ABC Model, you now have a systematic approach that will always make you more successful and provide with you an immunity to anything else that's happening in the world around you. You won't rely on the outside world

to make you happy. You now have your own system for increasing your happiness. You have no control over what happens in the world around you, but you can always transform yourself.

When you make these small, quarterly improvements in how you spend your time, Day 90 of your quarter will be significantly better than Day 1, and this can be the case for you every quarter. There are always surprising new things you can see, plan, and achieve during each 90-day period.

No more Irritating or Okay.

Tasks and responsibilities that have always frustrated you and drained you of energy can now disappear. And the changes will not only be meaningful to you but measurable and observable by others.

I think anybody who knows me would be able to look at me and say that I've really improved over the years in how I'm spending my time and that, these days, I seem to be continually in a good mood. This is the result of lots of improvements in the way I spend my time, often in the form of teamwork that I've worked out with other people where I'm doing only the activity in that teamwork that really fascinates me.

At the same time, everyone around me is doing only the parts of the teamwork that fascinate them. When a role exists that no one finds fascinating, that's when you need to look at hiring someone new who will be fascinated by it, or else look at automating the activity.

When you're in an organization where no one is doing anything irritating or okay, the positive effects on relationships, teamwork, and energy are profound.

Five improvements every 90 days.
No matter how much progress you've already made, at the beginning of every quarter, set a goal of five new improvements you can make to shift your time into C.

Human beings are not static, and neither is the world around us. When I shift something for myself from A to C or from B to C, there's immediately an impact on the individuals around me, and the conversation must continue so that everyone stays on the fascinating path.

Life can become very complicated by technological, economic, and psychological factors. But the only conversation I want to have inside my organization is, "How much time are you spending on A, on B, and on C, and how would you like to shift those in the next 90 days?" Someone else's shift might involve them doing more work with technology, while mine involves spending more time exploring new ideas in conversation. As long as everyone is working in their area of fascinating, the important things will be covered.

100 quarters x compound growth.
Every quarter, you'll shift your time and activity toward fascinating in five ways. These are permanent improvements, and the improvements you make next quarter are going to be in addition to those, resulting in a compounding effect. In the third quarter, improvements will be built on the foundation of the improvements of the previous two quarters.

There will be a multiplication effect from this process because thinking, communication, decision-making, action, and teamwork accelerate based on progress. Each of these starts with you but moves on to include a greater number of others on your team: You do one thing, and then 100 things happen outside of you.

You can treat the idea of multiplying every quarter as a normal thought, but you can't multiply normally if most of your activity and time is involved in irritating and okay activities. You can only multiply normally if you have the sense that, at the end of every quarter, more and more of your time is being spent in your area of fascinating.

We're in a turnover phase in the world right now where if you don't have something you're fascinated with to make a living by, you're going to disappear. The ABC Model is a clear-cut resolution to this, a way to achieve personal growth in a technological world.

Fascinating gets more fascinating.
You'll never run out of new things to be fascinated with, and your overall sense of fascination will keep deepening and expanding within The ABC Model.

This is part of exponential thinking, and I'm personally experiencing this now, in my seventies. Most people think that things drop off with age, that you're more focused on nostalgia and that you aren't looking forward to the type of growth you used to look forward to. For me, things are actually much better because I have the benefit of 73 years of experience, and I've realized that I have to eliminate certain things from my life.

I've learned lessons and improved particular skills, and I'm convinced that my life 25 years from now will be even better than it is today. There's only one route to get there: As fast as I can, I have to get all my time and activity into the realm of fascinating. In doing so, the fascinating things of next quarter are going to be more fascinating than the fascinating things of this quarter.

Conclusion
Multiplying Is The Reward
You keep growing faster and becoming friction-free when others are slowing down and stopping.

One activity that falls into my "irritating" category is meetings. Unless the agenda is specifically laid out in advance and everyone attending is well prepared, I find meetings to be a waste of my time. And so I've put into practice a policy that I won't participate in meetings that don't meet certain criteria. In this way, I've implemented changes that will make my life increasingly more enjoyable and fascinating.

This is just one example of how, by telling the truth about how I feel and taking control, I've improved my life in a specific way—and you have the same ability to improve your own life.

Your energy always spreads outward.
With The ABC Model, you're taking full responsibility for changing your personal situation to the maximum degree, which causes your energy to jump. You're going to be incredibly more pleasant to be around, and people are going to get energized by being around you simply because you've taken 100 percent accountability and are continually making the changes that make you a much easier person to communicate, cooperate, and create with.

You'll see this happen in every situation that involves other people. The energy you put out there will give others energy to make the same shift too. Your fascination and motivation will motivate them.

Every project is simpler and easier.
Fundamental to The ABC Model is that you're always making things better, for yourself and for those around you. When you work in teamwork with people who are also operating in their own areas of fascinating and motivating, things become simple and friction-free. Because no one on the team is stuck doing irritating or okay activities, the energy, creativity, and excitement that each person brings to the project makes it go faster, without any snags in the process.

Some people might think that the more people involved in a project, the more complex it becomes. But when everyone is doing only what they love and do best, contributing to the project in a way that fascinates and motivates them, there's nothing to slow them down. It's when you have fewer people involved, and they have to do parts of the project they find irritating, that friction and drag occur.

Time keeps slowing and expanding.
Since I started using The ABC Model and operating more and more in my area of fascinating activities, I've noticed that time seems to slow down. Single days are like universes in themselves, and every week seems very full in terms of how much I'm able to get done. This is in contrast to doing irritating or okay activities, which we all tend to want to get through as quickly as possible.

The more your time and activity are free from irritating and okay, the more you enjoy your time and don't want to rush through it. You have a greater appreciation for each new experience because you always have more than enough time to connect and enjoy the fresh insights you gain.

During your more and more fascinating life, you'll find yourself living increasingly in the present instead of spending your time looking ahead to when you'll be doing something that isn't irritating or just okay.

Start to finish with just three circles.

As you use this model, your confidence about encountering every new development in the world around you keeps growing because you immediately process it in terms of what's irritating, okay, and fascinating to you. You're always connected to your emotional reactions, and that's what you use to make decisions about what you'll be involved in.

The visual representation of The ABC Model is simple. It's not pages of diagrams; it's just three circles. If you understand these three circles, you understand how to use The ABC Model. The circles represent all of your time and activity, and the point of the system is to end up with just one circle: Fascinating.

Because the world is always changing, there are going to be new things every quarter that you find irritating or okay. As you become accustomed to using The ABC Model, you'll immediately notice these things, take action, and come up with changes to delegate, automate, or eliminate them. It will become a habit. And the irritating and okay activities you transform this quarter are ones you'll never have to deal with again.

Transforming everything you encounter.

Every time you transform irritating into fascinating, your life gets better. Your always-expanding mastery of The ABC Model means that everything around you improves regardless of the circumstances you're in.

My aim is to improve not just my own situation, but my

team's as well. In growing our organization, I'm very aware of the impact I have on every team member. I want the company to grow. I want people to count working here among the best experiences of their lives. And I know that the more each person is working in their area of fascinating, the happier they'll be, and the better our results will be.

Working only in your area of fascinating activities isn't an unachievable dream. There has been enormous practical and material progress in the world such that people can be freed up from the tasks that irritate them and drain their energy. Life doesn't have to be a grind. More and more of the world is moving beyond that.

Contrary to generally-held opinion, we don't have to accept that there are irritating tasks that everyone just has to do. As entrepreneurs, we're in a position to step back and look at how we're spending our time, divide up our activities in terms of our emotional response to them, and make changes and improvements that allow us to spend more of our time doing only the things that fascinate and motivate us. And we're able to implement a system in our businesses whereby everyone is able to do the same.

By using The ABC Model to make this a reality, quarter after quarter, we can live happier, more engaged lives and free ourselves up to create and innovate in ways that benefit everyone around us.

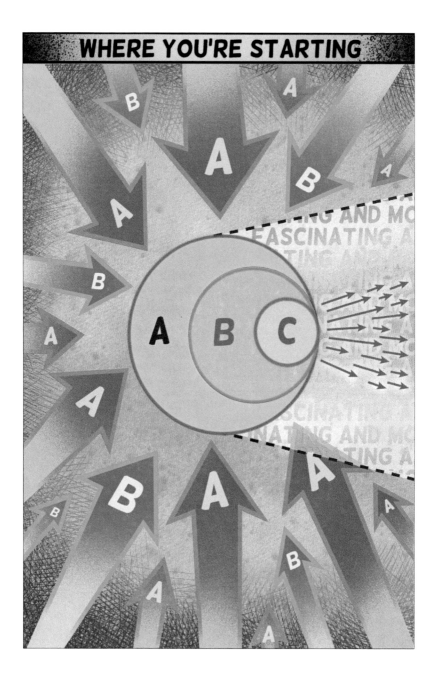

WHERE YOU'RE STARTING

The Strategic Coach Program
Expanding Entrepreneurial Freedom

The Strategic Coach Program, launched in 1989, has qualifications, measurements, structures, and processes that attract a particular type of talented, successful, and ambitious entrepreneur.

One differentiating quality of these Strategic Coach participants is that they recognize that the technology-empowered 21st century is a unique time to be an entrepreneur. It's the first time that a growing number of individuals with no special birth privileges and no special education can achieve almost anything they set their minds to.

These self-motivated individuals who participate in the three levels of Strategic Coach accept that if they can focus on mastering the right mindsets, they can experience increasing breakthroughs for themselves, both personally and professionally, that are new in history.

The ABC Model is one of these breakthrough mindsets, and there are dozens more for you to master.

Mindsets that enable entrepreneurs to escape.
Many entrepreneurs have the potential and the willingness to achieve exponential goals in the 21st century, but they are blocked from taking action and making progress because they feel trapped in three ways:

• **Trapped thinking:** They are isolated by their own disconnected creativity, which continually churns out ideas that don't translate into achievement. *At Strategic Coach, entrepreneurs increasingly liberate their thinking to create* *entirely new practical breakthroughs for themselves and others.*

• **Trapped circumstances:** They are surrounded by people who don't support their ambitions, who actively oppose them, or who try to make them feel guilty about their achievements and dreams. *At Strategic Coach, entrepreneurs learn how to increasingly surround themselves with like-minded and like-motivated individuals in every area of their personal and business lives.*

• **Trapped energy:** They're using much of their daily energy to simply sustain themselves without ever actually experiencing exponential performance and results. They wanted to create a growing business but it turns out that they've only created a job—one that always stays the same. *At Strategic Coach, entrepreneurs continually transform every part of their business organizations so that they become self-managing, and then self-multiplying.*

Mindsets that enable entrepreneurs to achieve.
Around the world, the vast majority of entrepreneurs never get out of these trapped circumstances, but at Strategic Coach, our participants not only escape from these limitations, they also jump to extraordinary levels of achievement, success, and satisfaction.

They never stop growing. Strategic Coach participants continually transform how they think, how they make decisions, how they communicate, and how they take action based on their mastery of dozens of unique entrepreneurial mindsets that have been developed in the Program. These are purely entrepreneurial mindsets, like The ABC Model.

We've taken a look at what goes on in the minds of the best entrepreneurs and have created a thinking system that is custom-designed for them and adjusts to the ambition of each individual.

The Strategic Coach Program provides an accelerating lifetime structure, process, and community for these entrepreneurs to create exponential breakthroughs.

Mindsets that enable entrepreneurs to multiply.
Depending on where you are right now in your life and business, we have a complete set of entrepreneurial mindsets that will immediately jump you up to the next level in terms of your ambition, achievements, and progress. Over the course of your entrepreneurial lifetime, you can move upward through our three levels of mindset measurement and scoring:

1. The Strategic Coach Signature Program: From isolation to teamwork. At this first breakthrough level, you create a "Unique Ability Team" in which everyone does only what they love and do best, allowing you to have a "Self-Managing Company" where your business runs successfully without your having to be involved in the day-to-day operations. Every successful entrepreneur dreams about having this kind of teamwork and organization. Through the Signature level of the Program, these dreams become a reality.

2. The 10x Ambition Program: From teamwork to exponential. You make breakthroughs that transform your life, and your organization becomes a "Self-Multiplying Company." Talented entrepreneurs want to free their biggest growth plans from non-supportive relationships, situations, and circumstances. Through the 10x Ambition level of Strategic Coach, their biggest aspirations attract multiplier capabilities, resources, and opportunities.

3. The Game Changer Jump Program: From exponential to transformative. As your entrepreneurial life becomes exponential, your Self-Multiplying Company become transformative. *The key evidence of this is that your biggest competitors want to become your best students, customers, and promoters.* Game Changer entrepreneurs in Strategic Coach become the leading innovators and cutting-edge teachers in their industries and continually introduce new strategies, methods, and systems that create *new* industries.

Measure yourself, score yourself, get started.

We've created an ABC Model Scorecard you can use to score yourself according to the eight mindsets discussed in this book. Go to *strategiccoach.com/go/abcmodel* to download your copy. Read through the four statements for each mindset and give yourself a score of 1 to 12 based on where your own mindset falls on the spectrum. Put each mindset's score in the first column at the right, and then add up all eight and put the total at the bottom. Now, think about what scores would represent progress over the next quarter. Write these in the second scoring column, add them up, and write in the total.

When you compare the two scores, you can see where you want to go in terms of your achievements and ambitions. If this fast exercise tells you that you want to multiply in all these areas, contact us today to get started:

The Strategic Coach Program is ready for you! Visit us online at *strategiccoach.com* or call us at 416.531.7399 or 1.800.387.3206.

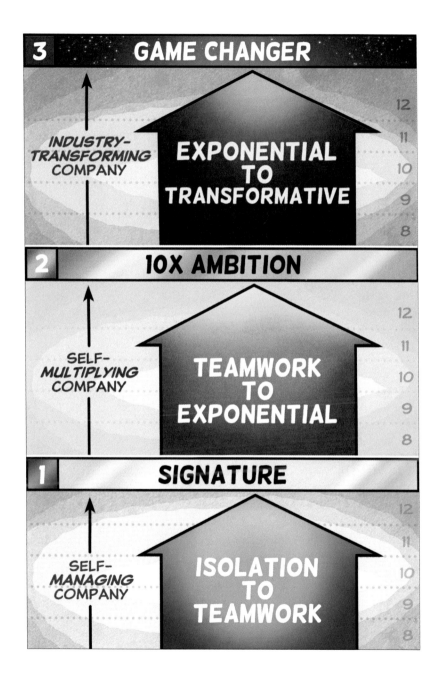

The ABC Model Breakthrough Scorecard

Turn the page to view the Scorecard and read through the four statements for each mindset. Give yourself a score of 1 to 12 based on where your own mindset falls on the spectrum. Put each mindset's score in the first column at the right, and then add up all eight and put the total at the bottom.

Then, think about what scores would represent progress for you over the next quarter. Write these in the second scoring column, add them up, and write in the total.

When you compare the two scores, you can see where you want to go in terms of your achievements and ambitions.

Mindsets	1	2	3	4	5	6
1 — Three Circle Breakthrough	Your whole business career has been almost entirely irritating, frustrating, and complicated — and you don't see it improving.			You'd love to have a better way to deal with constant change in your business life, but you don't have a mental map for doing this.		
2 — Emotionally Alert And Decisive	You notice that you're so bogged down with energy-draining problems that you've lost touch with how you're actually feeling.			You're convinced that the way most people approach business leaves out a lot of who you are, but you don't know how to operate in a better way.		
3 — Eliminate Everything Irritating	You're so buried in things you don't like doing that it's impossible for you to even imagine things being any different in the future.			You know that a lot of what you do every day is a waste of energy, but you don't understand how to escape from these situations.		
4 — Delegating "Okay"	You've never had any expectations that your business activity would be stimulating — just making a living is all you've ever wanted.			You're increasingly worried that five years from now, your work will be the same routine as today. You can't see where the breakthrough is.		
5 — Expanding Fascinating (And Motivating)	You're totally convinced that anything that was exciting about your career — and there hasn't been much — is all in the past.			You've identified the area where you always feel energized, but you lack the support system that will enable you to spend more time there.		
6 — Tell The Truth Every 90 Days	You know that the truth about your business is that everything is always going to get worse for you and everyone you're working with.			You can see what's working for you and what isn't, but you're frustrated because you don't have a strategy for making systematic improvement.		
7 — Growth Formula For Everyone	You don't have any time, attention, or resources to spend on making the work of your employees more enjoyable. This will never happen.			You love being in teamwork where everybody loves what they're doing, but it's a mystery to you how to increase this experience.		
8 — 100 ABC Quarterly Jumps	You have only one goal: to make as much money as possible and retire as soon as possible. Nothing else interests you at this point.			You've had glimpses of how much bigger and better your future could be, but it's hard to bring that future vision into the present.		
Scorecard	➡	➡	➡	➡	➡	➡

7	8	9	10	11	12	Score Now	Score Next
You know what the structures and processes of your industry are and you use best practices to run a successful business.			You continually organize your past, present, and future by transforming all of your activity according to three kinds of emotional responses.				
Your attitude about business success is that it's strictly about the numbers. You know which ones are important and you're on top of them.			You're increasingly alert to what your emotions are telling you about the best improvements you can make right now.				
You learned very early in your career to be the master of everything you don't like doing and to make sure you do unpleasant things first.			You accept that anything that irritates you will always be a waste of your energy — and you immediately work to eliminate it.				
Your whole success so far has been based on making your daily business life as impersonal, routine, and emotionless as possible.			You recognize that any situation that merely has "okay" energy is always a great project for permanent delegation and automation.				
You see yourself as someone who accepts things as they are and who has learned to put up with things that are annoying and boring.			You identify, integrate, and continually expand every activity in your life that will increasingly fascinate and motivate you in the future.				
You have a job and so does everyone else in your company. No one gets paid unless everyone peforms according to their job description.			You use each three-month period of your life to move any time spent in "irritating" and "okay" into the "fascinating" zone.				
You know that in the future, just having a good job is going to be a big deal for everyone, and that's what you're already providing.			You continually master The ABC Model for yourself while also teaching an increasing number of others how to do it.				
You know that the future is so uncertain in your industry that you have no idea what your business will look like ten years from now.			Your excitement about this quarter's ABC Model Breakthrough increases your commitment to doing this for 25 years.				
⇨ ⇨ ⇨ ⇨			⇨ ⇨ ⇨ ⇨				

About The Author
Dan Sullivan

Dan Sullivan is the founder and president of The Strategic Coach Inc. and creator of The Strategic Coach® Program, which helps accomplished entrepreneurs reach new heights of success and happiness. He has over 40 years of experience as a strategic planner and coach to entre- preneurial individuals and groups. He is author of over 30 publications, including *The 80% Approach*™, *The Dan Sullivan Question*, *Ambition Scorecard*, *Wanting What You Want*, *The 4 C's Formula*, *The 25-Year Framework*, *The Game Changer*, *The 10x Mind Expander*, *The Mindset Scorecard, The Self-Managing Company*, *Procrastination Priority*, and *The Gap And The Gain*, and is co-author with Catherine Nomura of *The Laws of Lifetime Growth*.

Made in the USA
Las Vegas, NV
05 January 2022

40309488R00048